Entrepreneurial Spirit
Dream Big, Do Bigger

MAX CHAHUA

DEDICATION

To my beloved family.

CONTENTS

ACKNOWLEDGMENTS

To all the people who positively influenced my life

INTRODUCTION

When the great explorers, like Magellan, Columbus, made explorations to the new world they called it "Enterprise".

The synonym or meaning of Enterprise was Adventure.

This spirit of adventure continues in millions of people who have an idea, and want to turn it into a business.

Entrepreneurship is the spirit that allowed the discovery of America, it is the spirit that today allows the creation of new products and services.

And it is the spirit we need to get to Mars and to conquer the solar system.

The spirit that lies in every entrepreneur who armed with a dream, wishes to achieve success, giving value to millions of people.

It is the entrepreneurs who shape our society, giving jobs, services and products to thousands or millions of people.

It is the entrepreneurs who have an idea, decide to

implement it and take risks to achieve success.

In this book we will talk about entrepreneurship, how to be a successful entrepreneur, we will talk about business, how to be a successful entrepreneur.

We will talk about the characteristics an entrepreneur needs to have.
And the mental focus necessary to achieve success.

The importance of entrepreneurship, skills and knowledge necessary for the entrepreneur, some business statistics.

In these times of great change, it is important to take into account the issue of entrepreneurship.

Entrepreneurship is not easy, and much less is doing business, and making it profitable.

In fact the statistics are against us, regardless of the country, the statistics are similar, on average 8 or 9 out of 10 businesses fail in the first 5 years.

What makes one entrepreneur different from another?
What makes one successful entrepreneur and not another?

The answer is not simple, and it has many variables.

This book deals with these questions, and answers them, we will briefly say that a factor for an entrepreneur to be successful are managerial skills, that is, the ability of the person to be able to set up groups, control cash flow, create business plans and start them.

Also to be successful it is necessary to have soft skills such as vision, ability to delay gratification, perseverance, ability to adapt, ability to learn quickly, ability to solve problems.

We will talk about momentum and innovation.
We will also mention who are the entrepreneurs, what they do different from most people.
What is needed to be part of this group and the mindset necessary to achieve success in this area.

Let me tell you a short story, before we start: My story.
I was just starting a new project.
And doubts and fears began to assail me, internal fears that told me "maybe I won't make it", "it's difficult", "there are many obstacles", "I don't have enough money", "It's too much work", "there are many things I don't know"
These phrases that I repeated to myself were subconscious, not that I was saying it consciously, but I was doing it unconsciously.
I realized, that my progress began to decrease, my fears began to grow, my doubts also, and that was also reflected in my progress, my progress began to slow down, my discipline diminished and so did my motivation.

I was blocked for several days, I thought, I had the same desire to achieve my goals, but it was not true. or at least it was not reflected in my progress, and also as I explain my motivation and discipline was on the floor.

However, I like to follow successful people on social networks, to see that I can model them.
And just one of these successful people that I follow did

a LIVE streaming through his social networks, and in it he invited a friend who was a millionaire and successful.

He said many important things, that made me realize where I was failing.

But the most important thing that I remember is what he said, and I will write next:

"Things are created in the world 2 times, first in your mind and then in reality."

Although I had heard these phrases several times, in authors like Robert Kiyosaki or T. Harv. Eker, I had totally forgotten them.

This person mentioned that there were millions of people who did not achieve financial freedom, or the life they wanted because they saw it as something distant, unattainable.

He said it was bullsh*t.

That we can all achieve financial freedom and the life that we want.

But if you believe that something is unattainable, due to this law, that everything is created in the world 2 times, people seeing it unattainable would give up their dreams and goals.

Hearing I said to myself, "no wonder this guy is a millionaire, what a mentality."

Then I reminded myself, why I was doing this endeavor, what I wanted to achieve, and I realized that I was letting myself beat by obstacles.

Since this endeavor was very difficult for me, because I was basically thinking from scratch.

I was also letting myself be overcome by my doubts and fears.

To which I remembered, when I had a similar situation several years ago:

And it was when I was a trainee in a company as a business consultant, the work was difficult, demanding, and tiring, after several months, I decided to quit, due to how demanding it was.

But later I regretted this decision, as it was a good opportunity to earn more income and grow financially.

The following year, I had another opportunity to become a trainee at another company.

After all that year, I realized that my mistake was my lack of vision, as I said the job was demanding, I had to promote financial products to clients, I was rejected when selling

these products, I had to walk for several hours to offer these products, all these things little by little, made me forget why I started working in that company.

And I had done it for 2 reasons, one was to grow financially, since after the training my income would increase, and the other was that I could gave value to people, that is, I advised and guided clients so that they can achieve their goals financial

The pressure, the fatigue, the physical and mental exhaustion, and finally the lack of vision made me give up on the first company.

When I realized all this, when I entered this new company,

I decided that no obstacle, or anything mentioned above, was going to stop me, I was focused on my goal and I was going to achieve it.

After several months, of struggle and work, I was finally able to pass the trainee training.

And I realized, that the same was for this endeavor, if one has vision (in addition to persistence, discipline, courage, motivation), there will be no one who can stop you.

I was letting myself be overcome by my fears, and remembering that "things are created 2 times first in your mind and then in reality"

They made me realize that my fears were creating my reality.

So I promised myself that fear, or fatigue, or ignorance would never stop me, that I was going to focus on my goal and I was going to achieve it, if I didn't know something I was going to learn it, if it was tired I was going to do it anyway.

I had a clear goal in mind.

I promised myself that I would not doubt myself and my abilities.

In this book, I invite you to invoke your entrepreneurial spirit.

I invite you to meet this world of business and entrepreneurship, a new world, full of wealth and abundance.

Like Columbus and other explorers!! Welcome to a world full of adventure and risk called Entreprise !!!

WHY THIS BOOK IS CALLED ENTREPRENEURIAL SPIRIT

It is called this way, because the top 10% who control 76% of the wealth in the United States are entrepreneurs.

An entrepreneur is in turn an internal investor.

Entrepreneurs create their company, take risks, invest in it, make it grow, and when it becomes large enough, they make an IPO (Initial Public Offering), selling their shares to the public, creating wealth for all the actors involved in this process.

Unlike the majority, these entrepreneurs SELL their shares while most people BUY these shares.

As sellers, and not shareholders, they can generate millions by selling IPO shares, and subsequently, generate many more millions by issuing shares.

.

It is the entrepreneurs, along with the investors, who shape true capitalism, they are the ones who take risks, take an idea, and with work, dedication, focus and effort, create assets from scratch, which provide services and products to society.

Which are then sold to millions of people, generating wealth and value for thousands and millions of people.

This book focuses on how this group thinks, the skills they possess or must possess to be successful, the mental structure necessary to think like an entrepreneur, the knowledge they need to succeed as entrepreneurs, and the tools they have to be successful in this complicated, but at the same time very rewarding business world.

ENTREPRENEURSHIP

Entrepreneurship is basically identifying opportunities, and organizing the resources to take that opportunity.

It is the ability to take risks, and take challenges.

It is to innovate and exploit our creativity to the maximum.

Entrepreneurship is an attitude, which allows you to turn your dreams into reality.

It is taking an idea and looking for the tools to make it come true.

An entrepreneur is a person, eager to progress, who seeks to solve a problem, has confidence in himself, overcomes challenges, adapts to change, and takes risks to achieve his goals.

An entrepreneur fights against adversity, in order to develop his idea, he/she has to develop new skills and strengths, and he/she needs to make use of new tools.

All entrepreneurship is born from an idea, which can later generate economic benefit.

The entrepreneur can take advantage of the change and take it as an opportunity.

According to the RSA (Royal Spanish Academy), entrepreneurship is,
"To undertake and start a work, a business, an endeavor, especially if they involve difficulty or danger".

DIFFERENCE BETWEEN ENTREPRENEUR AND BUSINESSMAN

After researching the difference between an entrepreneur and a Businessman, I started to get dizzy due to the different definitions they give of both.
However, I was able to conclude the following:

-An entrepreneur is a person who tries to get his idea forward, and in this he puts all his effort and energy. (He is mainly committed to the project and to make it work)

-A businessman on his part is a person, who seeks to develop a business that is economically viable, delegates, works as a team.

Given these definitions, it could be said that the entrepreneur is a person who is starting in the business world, and who seeks to carry out his idea or project. In some cases, using innovative ideas.

For his part, a businessman is a person with more tools available to him, he can count on workers, creates business plans, seeks to make the business profitable.

In summary, it could be said that the entrepreneur is the evolved version of the entrepreneur, has more tools and relies on knowledge and skills such as business plans and work personnel.

Every businessman is an entrepreneur, or at some point he was.

However, not every entrepreneur is a businessman, since on his way to get his idea forward, he may or may not succeed.

In the event that he initially succeeds in this first stage of an idea or project, he would become a businessman.

Before which, due to the need, to systematize and make his idea profitable, he is forced to become a businessman.

And he has to develop business plans, delegate, take over labor, to make profitable what was his idea or project at the beginning.

It could be said that a businessman is an entrepreneur who was successful with his idea or business, so he must evolve because his idea is successful, he needs to develop systems, hire staff, develop business plans, work as a team, learn new skills managerial and managerial.

This is the definition we will use in the book and on pages ahead.

I emphasize it here because when I investigated the differences between entrepreneur and businessman, I found many definitions.
These definitions are the product of my conclusions after reviewing different definitions available.

Another way of saying it is that the entrepreneur is the caterpillar, who is in the process of change, and in the process of making his idea or project successful.
The businessman is the butterfly, who has more tools (wings), to be able to make his idea economically viable, making use of managerial tools, such as hiring staff, drawing up business plans, delegating, etc.

COUNTRIES FRIENDLY WITH ENTREPRENEURSHIP

According to The Global Entrepreneurship Monitor, one of the most important studies that are carried out on entrepreneurship.

The National Entrepreneurship Context Index (NECI) mentions the most entrepreneur-friendliness countries, for 2019-2020.

The 5 most entrepreneurial friendly countries are:
1- Switzerland
2- Holland
3- Qatar
4- China
5- UAE
6- India
10- USA
23 - Mexico

China is ranked 4th, India 6th, and USA 10th.

This study indicates those countries that are friendlier to entrepreneurship and provide better coverage and conditions to undertake.

This study says:

"Entrepreneurship is an essential driver of the health and

wealth of a country, and also an engine of formidable growth ... many governments of the world see entrepreneurship as a key, in the solution to end poverty and social inequity "mentions this 2019-2020 report in its executive summary.

As we can see, China has been making progress in recent years in this index.

SOME STATISTICS ON BUSINESS AND ENTREPRENEURSHIP

LEVEL OF JOB SATISFACTION

After having reviewed job satisfaction in various countries, I mention some data:

The main reasons for job dissatisfaction are:
- Low wages
- Job instability (which has been growing in recent years)
- Bad work schedule

In the United States, the Conference Board prepares an annual Job Satisfaction survey

Now in the midst of a covid pandemic, the Randstad Monitor produced a job satisfaction survey for 2020, including the following topics:

-% of people who feel supported by their employers
-% of people who had trouble learning new skills to adapt to the pandemic.
-% of people, who feel they have the materials to face digitization
-% of workers who would accept a leave or reduction of working hours.

-% of workers who would accept a lower salary

-% of workers who would accept an increase in their working hours without an increase.

-% of people who would like to work from home

As we can see, the pandemic brought new changes, and among them adapting to this "new normal" is very important.

After having reviewed job satisfaction from various sources, it ranges from 60 to 70% in developed countries, with the lowest job satisfaction in Japan at 40%.

According to the 2019 Randstad Workmonitor, India has the highest job satisfaction with 86%, followed by Mexico 82%, USA with 78%, Brazil 77%, China 74%, Chile 75%, Japan 43%.

If a worker has job stability and is satisfied with his work, he may not have the need to start a business.

On the other hand, if job satisfaction decreases, and job instability increases, many people will be forced to undertake.

Since there are 2 reasons to undertake:
-Entrepreneurship out of necessity
-Entrepreneurship by opportunity

Being an entrepreneur on the other hand is not easy, and there is a high risk of bankruptcy, a statistic that we will share below.

SURVIVAL OF PRIVATE SECTOR COMPANIES

FOR THE NEXT 10 YEARS

According to the Bureau of Labor Statistics' Business Employment Dynamics, here's what the survival rate looks like:

About 78% of businesses with employees will survive their first year in business. (The most recent data shows that, of the small businesses that opened in March 2019, 78% made it to March 2020.)

About 68.2% of businesses with employees will survive their second year in business. (The recent data shows that of the small businesses that opened in March of 2018, 68.2% made it to March of 2020.)

About 50% of businesses with employees will survive their fifth year in business. (Data shows that of the small businesses that opened in March of 2015, 50% made it to March of 2020.)

About 34% of businesses will survive their 10th year in business. (The most recent data shows that of the small businesses that opened in March of 2010, 34.3% made it to March of 2020.)

So the odds, are basically against us. ¡¡Just 34% of business will survive their 10th year!!

What makes a business successful?

What can we do to reduce the odds against us, and improve the odds in our favor?

ENTREPRENEURSHIP VS INNOVATION

As I mentioned according to the Royal Spanish Academy, entrepreneurship is:

"To undertake and start a work, a business, an endeavor, especially if they contain difficulty or danger"

and innovation according to the RAE:

"Creation or modification of a product, and its introduction in a market"

In other words, while undertaking is starting a work, or business, or putting our idea into action, it does not necessarily have to be something new, or different, for example, it could start doing traditional businesses such as a restaurant, a minimarket, etc.

For its part, innovate is to do something different, or modify something existing, for example in the case of restaurants, you could do something new, for example a restaurant where your products contain quinoa, or maca.

In the minimarket sector, for its part, it could make a minimarket that sells only organic products or something like that, or that has another form of customer service, among others.

Not all entrepreneurs are innovative.
Since they can undertake traditional businesses without the need to create a new product or modify it.

Not all entrepreneurs are successful in their introduction of an idea or product, and as we can see, part of the definition of innovation implies its introduction to the market.

Nor does not all innovation imply entrepreneurship, since there may be innovation in existing companies, when creating new products or lines of business, or a new form of distribution or customer service.

INNOVATIVE BUSINESSES

However, an entrepreneur who in turn has an innovative idea, can generate value to society.

Such is the case, for example, of startups in the technology sector.

Cases for example of recent technology companies such as: WhatsApp, Youtube, Facebook, Instagram and Twitch.

These new innovative ventures, managed to achieve success, brought new business models to the market and managed to create jobs, and thousands of people who earn thousands of dollars using their platforms.

Innovative companies can create high impact, in a country, in its economy and benefit thousands of people by giving value to their customers and users.

Many ventures were born from a garage, like Apple.

His founder Steve Jobs, at that time was a young leader, with big dreams and ideas, had vision and wanted to create an innovative company that would improve the lives of Americans.

At a time, it became the most valued company in the United States.

Today it remains one of the largest companies in the United States.

The founders of these innovative companies have to have different qualities, as for example in the case of Steve Jobs, he was an excellent communicator and salesperson, and was able to inspire people.

When he promoted his products, like the case of the iphone, ipad, ipod, he did it so well, that he made everyone want to buy Apple products.

He, too, was an inspiring leader, and was able to transmit his vision to his work team, and to his clients, who, more than buying a product, were buying a dream, a vision.

ADAM SMITH AND THE WEALTH OF THE NATIONS, ORIGIN OF WORK AND BUSINESS

Adam Smith, in his book The Wealth of Nations talks about the division of labor, and in it tells an example that of the pin factory.

He mentions that the author himself could only make 1 pin a day, but like this factory, it has its functions divided into branches, that is, each person has a specific function (one makes the cuts, one is dedicated to filing, another enamels it, etc.).

By dividing the work of making a pin into 18 different operations, where a worker did 2 or 3 operations in the business.

These 10 people on average, due to the division of labor, could make 48,000 pins a day.

But if everyone did it for their part, maybe they could make 20 pins a day, or maybe just 1.

This division of labor, and the rise of factories, gave rise to the world's first workers.

Since prior to the industrial era, most people were farmers (they were entrepreneurs from their own land, that is, they invested their time and money in the land, and then they hoped to recoup their investment through the sale of their crops).

The author also mentions that this division of labor makes workers specialize more in their activity, finding ways to be more efficient and productive.

Making each individual specialize in his field, and become more expert.

This multiplication of production made the prices of inputs cheaper.

The author also mentions that this division of labor is only possible due to the size of the market.

In other words, nobody would dare to make 48,000 pins a day if only 2,000 people lived in his village.

Since I would have pins to spare every day.

While in the cities, due to the division of labor, people tended to specialize in their branches.
In the field, people have to apply themselves in all branches, because the division of labor was not feasible.

In other words, only in large cities could factories succeed, and promote the division of labor, which fostered the efficiency of the industry and an improvement in productivity.

This division of labor, which was only possible in the cities, allowed the entrepreneurs who owned it, to enrich themselves and some to become millionaires, while also making their workers a new incipient middle class.

Now, Adam Smith's book was written in 1776.

At that time, only a few cities reached a million inhabitants. And they were considered large cities such as: London, Calcutta, among others.

As of today, we not only have large cities but also megacities, that is, cities with more than 10 million inhabitants.

As I write globally, there are 47 megacities worldwide, and 70% of these are in Asia.

There are also more than 500 cities worldwide that exceed one million inhabitants.
Here is a short list of some megacities, and their populations:

1. Guangzhou-Shenzhen (48,600,000)
2. Tokyo-Yokohama (39,800,000)
3. Shanghai (31,100,000)
4. Jakarta (28,900,000)
5. Delhi (27,200,000)
6. Karachi (25,100,000)
7. Seoul (24,800,000)
8. Manila (24 100,000)
9.New York-New Jersey-Connecticut-Pennsylvania, (23,700,000)
10.Bombay (23,600,000)

Other megacities (in 2017, in alphabetical order):
-Bangalore, India

-Bangkok, Thailand
-Bogota Colombia
-Buenos Aires, Argentina.
-Calcutta, India
-Chennai, India
-Mexico City, Mexico
-Daca, Bangladesh
-Cairo, Egypt
-Istanbul, Turkey
-Johannesburg, South Africa
-Kinsasa, DR Congo
-Lagos, Nigeria
-Lahore, Pakistan
-Lima Peru
-London, Great Britain
-Los Angeles United States
-Moscow, Russia
-Nagoya, Japan
-Osaka-Kobe-Kyoto, Japan
-Paris France
-Beijing, China
-Rio de Janeiro Brazil
-Tehran, Iran
-Tianjin, China
-Xiamen, China

If in 1776, entrepreneurs could become rich, due to the division of labor and large cities.

Almost 400 years later, in a globalized world, with 500 cities with more than 1 million inhabitants, and 57 megacities, entrepreneurs can become billionaires.

And even more, in an interconnected village, a person can sell their products or services through the internet, bypassing the barriers of distance.

The importance of language is also important, with English being the predominant language, which you can communicate with people from other countries (spoken by more than 2 billion native and non-native speakers in more than 25 countries), followed by Chinese (more than 1 billion of speakers), followed by Spanish (spoken by more than 500 million people in more than 21 countries).

Speaking of entrepreneurship, business and innovation.
Adam Smith had vision when he realized that the division of labor, specialization and large cities could create wealth in countries and in people.

But, could Adam Smith have imagined, more than 240 years later that the world would have 47 megacities, with more than 10 million inhabitants, making possible the existence of new millionaire and billionaire entrepreneurs?

If we compare the world today, with 200 years ago, we can realize the opportunities we have thanks to entrepreneurship and business, thanks to the internet and the interconnection between nations.

Platforms such as YouTube, Twitch, Facebook, among others, allow connecting thousands and millions of people of different nationalities, who communicate through English or the Spanish language.

If we see things in this way, we can realize that we are facing a world of great opportunities and possibilities.

I have a book called Passive Digital Income, where I mention how we can obtain 10 different types of passive income, through the internet, thanks to the birth of the information age. Taking advantage of this opportunity allows us to obtain income without having to work physically at all times, the work is done only once and then income or royalties are received from this work.

If you are interested, my book is in the Amazon store.

The internet was created in 1993, and today it keeps us interconnected, and it is a great opportunity for anyone who wants to take advantage of this powerful tool.

With the industrial age, the great entrepreneurs of factories and industries were born, many of whom became millionaires and billionaires.

With the internet, the great entrepreneurs of the information age were born and with it thousands of new billionaires.

THE STORY OF THE PUSS IN BOOTS

The story of Puss in Boots, is for me, the story of the businessman, who puts together various pieces (people, materials, capital, among others), and finally creates something magnificent with all of it, something that they could see in their mind that no one else more could.

This is the story of puss in boots:
The son of a miller receives a cat as an inheritance, laments his misfortune, and says that after eating the cat, he would have nothing left.
Hearing this (and to avoid being eaten), the cat very cleverly asks for a bag and a pair of boots, and with them, he joins things, situations, people, to finally achieve various objectives.
With great cunning, managing to turn a peasant into the Duke of Carabas, makes him the owner of the land and the castle of the ogre who is eaten in one bite.

Not bad for a cat, with boots!

The cat with great cunning and intelligence managed to make his lord very rich, and he does with intelligence and a pair of boots.

The story of Puss in Boots is the story of many entrepreneurs.

Many entrepreneurs, put things together, and shape businesses, companies and investments.
They find the:
- Investment
- Find or create a product or service
- Find investors
- Find qualified workers for each position
- They put together a system and manage it or delegate it to qualified people.

And they finally manage to create a great company with a great product or service, managed properly in each area.

And all this is born from an idea, a lot of cunning and the ability to negotiate, deal with people, sell and have excellent communication skills.

The book of Puss in Boots is for me an analogy of our subconscious, the Puss in Boots is our subconscious while the Duke of Carabas is each one of us, through our conscious mind.

As in the story of Puss in Boots, we can all achieve great things.

We only have to give our cat (our subconscious) a bag and a pair of boots, which in our days the bag would be, give

our subconscious knowledge through:
- Books, seminars, conferences, practices, games, simulations.

And a pair of boots, that is, give him some necessary tools to walk and let him walk so that he works in a fantastic way, you will see that your subconscious will create fabulous ideas, and that, accompanied, with a solid business plan or project, they can provide you with wealth and abundance in your life.

In the story, for the cat to operate it needs basic tools, such as a pair of boots and a bag, that is, for our subconscious to work in wonderful ways we must feed it with positive things, knowledge and skills.

Then with these few tools and a lot of cunning, the cat will achieve great feats, and finally make his master rich and important.

This is what characterizes a businessman and entrepreneur, his ability to solve problems, if he doesn't have the resources, he gets them, if he doesn't have the right personnel, he gets it, if he doesn't have the tools, he gets them.

CHARACTERISTICS ATTRIBUTED TO A BUSINESSMAN

Below is a list, which are commonly attributed to all successful entrepreneurs:

- -Vital force
- -Ingenuity
- -Vivacity
- -Generating principle that drives you to start great things
- -Ability to break paradigms
- -Ability to face risks
- -Ability to solve problems
- -Self-confidence
- -Ability to overcome challenges and opportunities
- -Ability to adapt to change
- -Patience
- -Ability to develop skills and knowledge to overcome obstacles
- -Ability to solve problems
- -Competence
- -leadership
- -teamwork
- -Organization
- -Service attitude
- -Vision
- -Ability to tolerate frustration
- -Persistence, and Consistency
- -Ability to self-motivate
- Self-confidence

-Discipline
-Planning of resources and activities
-Effectiveness, achieve more with less
-Achieve objectives
-Creativity
-Mind of abundance
-Administration and management skills.

As you can see, there are many characteristics that are attributed for a successful businessman or entrepreneur.

Above there are 30 characteristics.

However, if we follow the pareto principle, which indicates that 20% of what we do represents 80% of our success.

We will choose 20% of these characteristics that represent 80% of a successful entrepreneur.

20% of these 30 characteristics are 6, which I consider vital for success, you could choose your own 6 characteristics for success.

For me they are the following:

1- Vision - I consider this vital, since as I mentioned in my story, vision allows you to see the light at the end of the tunnel, and help you face the challenges that you have in front of you.
Great leaders have vision.

Columbus had a vision, when he wanted to get to India by circling the earth, in fact he never gave up his vision, he had patience and he never gave up on his goal in mind, he had to keep his vision for several years, until he was finally able to do it. reality.

2- Self-confidence - Self-confidence is vital for success, being sure of ourselves and our virtues and capabilities is important when undertaking, doing business and making decisions.

3-Self-motivation, Intrinsic Motivation - The word motivation comes from the Latin "motivus", which means movement, so that you can continue with your dreams, and keep "moving", you need a strong self-motivation, remember why you are wanting to achieve what you want.

4-Ability to solve problems- The ability to solve problems is very important, it is also linked to the ability to adapt, and develop skills and knowledge necessary to solve problems that occur to us.

This ability is essential for the life of every person, throughout our lives, we have always had obstacles that we have overcome.

For example, as children, a difficult problem for us was learning to read and write, today when we grow up it seems like a child's thing, but when we were little, these tasks for some of us could have been a colossal and difficult task to achieve.

As we grow, we face greater challenges and obstacles that force us to grow and expand our knowledge and skills.

5-Persistence and discipline- Both are important to be successful, the ability to continue and continue, when others are willing to quit is important for every entrepreneur.

Discipline, on the other hand, implies having to do things even if we do not have much desire that day, for example if we are sleepy, we still have to continue with our goal, or if we are lazy, even if we must continue with our objectives.

I once asked a successful person the following:
"How do you stay motivated, and not be demoralized when the going gets tough"

To which he replied:
The secret is this: "The key is that even if you are depressed or demoralized, you continue towards your goals, always focused on the path."

Once again, I said to myself: "I understand now why he is successful"

6- Planning and achieving objectives-
Planning is important, as it helps you remember and frame all of the above.

Planning allows you to see your goals, helps you reaffirm your vision, motivates you to face obstacles, allows you to be efficient, and also gives you feedback to see what things you can improve, or where you are failing.

Planning is important to organize your plan and remember your goals.
There is a phrase that says:

"10 minutes of planning is worth 1 hour of work."

Well, these are the 6 characteristics that I consider most important of an entrepreneur under the pareto principle, perhaps you can disagree with some that he mentioned but surely, we agree on several of these.

ENTREPRENEUR TOOLS

TOOL # 0: RELATIONS

Relations are very important. It is said that your income is the average of the five people around you.

I didn't understand the power of this tool until I put in into practice.
Face-to-face relationships are important but nowadays we can also create long distance relationships thanks to the internet.
I started to follow successful people in what I wanted to be. I started following successful people on Facebook, Instagram, YouTube.

I watched their webinars, their videos, their courses, I tried to model their mindset. Many of them showed their income in the businesses that I wanted to be successful. Several of these people were millionaires and had high income in the things that I wanted to be.

While watching their videos, I found powerful keys to the success of these people.

For example, one of them said: "Children do what they want, men do what they should."
He also said identify what Identify what is robbing you of energy and what gives you energy.

Again, I said, no wonder this guy is a millionaire.

I started to think about the things I did as a child, and I found a couple, one of them was doing leisure things at home that took 1 or 2 hours a day from me.

Seeing this powerful phrase from this successful person, I simply eliminated this distraction.

I uninstalled the source of my distraction, and did what he advised, "men do what they should."

I also realized that these distractions were robbing me energy.
And what gave me a lot of energy, was doing things I love, challenges I had to face, and things I had to learn to overcome these challenges.

Another successful character spoke of the mindset, that one attracts and creates the reality of him, that everything is energy and everything flows.

As everything is in motion and we all have an electromagnetic field, with which we attract or repel things.

If we have a weak mindset, people will perceive our energy, and they will feel doubts when it comes to doing business with us. If we have a powerful mindset people will feel attracted to do business with us.

Several of these characters spoke of security, vision, etc.

I also have several successful friends in various fields, with whom I occasionally meet in person.

Relationships are very important.

Donald Trump went bankrupt, in his autobiography he mentions that when he went to the streets he saw homeless people, and he realized that those homeless people were in a better financial position.

Because these homeless were at 0$, that is, they had no income, but neither debt.

While Trumo was $ -1.5 billion negative, due to the debts he had.

He managed to recover and then even be in a better financial position, due to his ability to solve problems **but also due to his relationships, relationships that he had managed to reap for many years.**

So it wasn't that difficult for him to raise capital. Because he had the connections, he had the right relationships to do great business.

Many of these successful people, when I spoke to them directly or when I saw them online, they said the same thing "Invest in your relationships, go to an expensive restaurant from time to time, stay in a luxury hotel if you have the possibility, since you can meet successful people there. " **Invest in your relationships**

TOOL # 1: BELIEVE IN YOURSELF

To be successful, you need confidence in yourself. Confidence in yourself and your abilities are vital for success, if I believe in myself, others will believe in me too.

If I don't believe in myself, how do I expect others to believe in me?

If you want to be successful you must act as if you have already arrived.

If you were a successful person, would you walk as you walk now, would you think as you think now, would you do what you currently do now?

Think of famous people maybe your favorite star, sports, or music, maybe some famous and famous person, listen to their lectures, their words, what they say about themselves, how they think, how they face adversity, challenges, what goals they have, you can learn a lot from these characters, since many of them have great goals, ambitions, dreams, which they plan to achieve within a certain period.

Believing in yourself, trusting in your own abilities, in your personal worth, is considered essential for personal success.

As they say, knowledge and skills add up, but attitude multiplies.

TOOL # 2: THE IMPORTANCE OF WORDS AND THOUGHTS

I remember when I worked in a company in the banking sector, when I started working, I had doubts and fears, I started in the world of sales by selling intangibles (loans to businesses and people).

My chief asked me, how I was regarding my goals.

And I said :

-I will try to reach my goal this week.

And he would say to me: "Will you try or will you do it?"

Realizing the strength of my thoughts and words I said:

"I'll do it."

Although it seems like a simple difference, there was a huge difference

By saying "I will do it" I was committing to give all my efforts to achieve my goal.

I also remember when I said:

"I think our client X bills 30,000 dollars a month"

To which he would say to me: "Do you think?"

To which he replied: "Our client X bills 30,000 dollars a month, here are the receipts"

At the beginning, as I mentioned to you, I started in the world of sales, with some doubts but as I gained clients, convincing them to acquire services, my confidence grew, I knew that what I was giving them was a service to improve their lives.

I truly believed that the service I gave benefited people, so I always prepared myself, and studied a lot, to try to give the best possible advice.

As you can see, words and thoughts are very important, since they shape our reality.

Words like "I will try", in some cases are used to say "I will not do it."

For example, when I called my friends to meet up, some would say "I'll try", it was a polite way of saying "I won't go", while other friends would say "I'll be there".

His commitment was reflected in his words.

The words we use shape our reality, words are the fuel for our brain, use weak words, and you will have a weak attitude. Use words and sentences that show determination and thus affect your mind.

Words and with them, speeches, have been used throughout the centuries, to inspire people, to motivate them, and even in times of war, to keep people with high morale, and high spirits,

As you can see, words shape our reality, in addition to allowing us to communicate with others through oral language.

To paraphrase Albus Dumbledore from Harry Potter: "Words are, our most inexhaustible source of magic, capable of inflicting damage as well as remedying it."

Or as Rafael Echevarría, author of "Ontology of language" says, "Language is not innocent."

Words you use, can be a powerful tool to empower yourself.

Through the words the determination of a person or the lack of it are reflected.

We have, for example:

SIR WINSTON CHURCHILL'S SPEECH:

"We will go to the end; we will fight in France; we will fight in the seas and oceans; we will fight with increasing confidence and increasing strength in the air; we will defend our island, whatever the cost; we will fight on the beaches; we will fight on the airfields; we will fight in the fields and in the streets; we will fight in the hills; we will never give up ... "

We can see in his words, the powerful determination that emerged from this great leader, he did not say "maybe, I will try, I will do what I can", **he said: "We will go to the end, we will fight and defend ourselves whatever the cost," We never give up".**

As was said at that time, Churchill mobilized the English language, and brought it to the battlefield, and that as we can see was no small thing.

This speech empowered millions of people to get the best out of themselves.

Also this other speech:

JOHN F. KENNEDY'S SPEECH:

"We have decided to go to the moon. We choose to go to the moon in this decade ..., **not because they are easy goals, but because they are hard**, because that challenge will serve to organize and measure the best of our energies and abilities, because that challenge it is a challenge that we are willing to accept, one that we do not want to postpone, and one that we will try to win ... "

What a speech! What a man! **"We have decided to go to the moon. We chose to go to the moon in this decade ..., not because they are easy goals, but because they are hard ..."**

These words empowered a country, made them dream, and put in their minds the goal of reaching the moon in that decade, the speech was delivered in September 1962, and the United States of America, reached the moon, in July 1969.

What leadership and what more ambitious goals.

What a leader!!

Remember that we are our words, we are what we think.

If you want to be great, think big, and use powerful words

TOOL # 3: UNDERSTAND LANGUAGE, BODY, AND EMOTION

The human being manages 3 domains, they are, language, body and emotion.

There must be coherence between them, for example, it would be incoherent for a person to say "I'm happy" with a dull and boring tone.

or say "I'm super happy" with a happy tone, but with the body crouched and hunched over.

What happens in one domain affects the other, and these 3, in turn, are necessary for learning.

For us to learn, learning must at least be handled in 2 domains.

Every businessman is careful with his words, emotions and thoughts, I have spoken with many successful entrepreneurs, they all agree on the same thing, **"Words and thoughts are powerful and shape our lives"**, **each one had a particular way of saying this, but they said more or less the same thing.**

For example, when sometimes I had meetings with some business friends, they made me notice the weakness in my words, when I said for example "I think that this month, I will not be able to reach this goal", always in their own way they told me to be very careful with my words, since they knew that words shape "my" reality, and they advised me to watch my thoughts, as they are vital for success.

They also explained to me about self-sabotage (our internal fears), they sabotage our lives and our goals, with weak and negative thoughts.

Many times the objectives and goals are within our reach, within our possibilities, but our weak thoughts, thoughts of smallness, limit us and do not allow us to perform and fulfill ourselves with our maximum potential.

Use strong words, phrases and speeches, words that enlarge your spirit, use motivational poems that help you achieve your goals and that you can develop your full potential, this is known by many entrepreneurs I deal with, which is why I find them very busy. and very motivated.

TOOL # 4: HABITS

"When we grow old, small habits become great tyrannies"

Gustave Flauvert

To be successful, you have to have a series of successful habits.

I put it this way, every time you perform an action, imagine that a thread is created in your mind, repeat it a thousand times, and you will have a thousand threads, maybe you can break 2,3,5, 20 threads, but 1,000, 10,000 threads is somewhat more complicated.

That's why if you have bad habits, they could be difficult to break. On the other hand, if they are good habits, your habits will anchor you to success.

In a hospital cancer patient were asked to quit smoking cigarettes. They were all aware of how withering and disastrous his bad smoking habit was. The warning was: "don't smoke anymore, stop smoking."

Did they quit? No.

Many of them had been smoking for 15-20 years.

It is difficult to change habits that we already have, since when we have habits, they form part of us, part of what we know, which is why it is easy to do these activities, and it does not require us to expend a lot of energy.

On the contrary, creating a new habit requires a lot of energy, 3-5 times more than that required for an already defined habit.

The brain does not like to waste energy, so it prefers to do things it knows, that is, it prefers to do things that we do in commonly and have it as a habit.

Well obviously if that bad habit is repeated in excess, excessively an causes damage to the person, it becomes an addiction, and is capable of destroying the person who has such addiction.

The mind likes to repeat things that produce pleasure, if for example, you like video games, you will want to repeat it from time to time.

The problem arises when you cannot control the amount of time you spend on something.

Knowing that the mind likes to repeat things that produce pleasure, and you want to stop smoking for

example, then you have to replace this habit with another that also produces pleasure.

You could, for example, in that time you used to do it to smoke, in this case dedicating yourself to something that you like and that gives you pleasure also, could be, for example, dancing, playing sports, meeting new friends, etc.

The brain also looks for a way to save energy, so the natural tendency is to turn almost any situation already experienced into a routine.

But the brain does not differentiate between good and bad habits.

To change habits, sometimes, some event of great importance to the person is needed.

For example:

-A father who is very distant and cold, decides to change when he sees that his son is the same.

-A sedentary person when he has a pre-heart attack.

On the other hand, the brain looks for situations that give it pleasure, therefore it is necessary to choose wisely what pleasures to have.

Another way that I consider simpler to change a habit is to change the environment.

I know a friend, who used to hang out at parties and discos, and he told me that he wanted to stop drinking alcohol, so I suggested him that instead of going to parties and discos that he go to church or sporting events, Which he said, NO, I want to stop drinking but still going to parties and discos.

Did he quit the bad habit? Obviously not.

Did he really want to quit from alcohol? Most likely not, maybe he was kidding me. Since he wasn't decided to quit from discos and parties, places were alcohol is everywhere.

So we have 3 options here, to acquire or stop bad habits.

1-change a bad habit that gives you pleasure, for another good habit that also gives you pleasure.

2-Remember an event of great importance in your life, due to a bad habit, and make the decision to make changes knowing that changing a habit is not easy.

3-Change your environment, attend courses where you learn something like a language, sport, skill, dance, meet people, or go to a park, library, community, or club where there is a group of people who have better

habits, or places where they have habits that you would like to have.

For example, it was enough for me to change my workplace to change some habits that I had when I was not working.

Remember that the universe does not like emptiness, so when you try to quit a bad habit, immediately that empty time you have to occupy it with something else productive, because if there is a vacuum, you will probably return to your bad habit.

Since you will not have anything else to do and you will return to what you know and that is not necessarily good or the best.

Now, what habits are considered useful and healthy?

I highlight some that I consider important for any person.

-Train and keep up to date, whether through books, seminars, audiobooks, conferences.

-Do sport

- Plan the day, the week, the month, the year, plan for the future.

-Write your goals.

-Create business plans, financial plans, retirement plans, etc. Plans, plans, plans.

- Set goals and objectives.

- Have a to-do list

-Participate in charity events, group, social and family events.

TOOL # 5: FINANCIAL STATEMENTS

There are, for example, many bankers and accountants, who know the subject of financial statements well and handle financial statements of other companies, but they never decided to keep an account of their own financial statements.

That is why the saying "In the blacksmith's house a wooden knife" is used many times, many times what they know is not applied to their own lives.

In order to have healthy finances, it is important that you take a look at your personal financial statements, you could, for example, abuse credit cards, go into debt, and put yourself at risk that your expenses are greater than your income, and this could make you sick, since worrying about paying bills often wears out a person physically and mentally.

There are many people who get sick and stressed, because they have many debts, and little income to face these debts, to which many nights of worry and insomnia arrive, thinking about how to pay those bills.

The financial statements are also important if you want, for example, to work in a company, or participate in a business, you must first assess whether it is good or not, but how can you know?

The answer is by looking at the Financial Statements of this company, if the company has good numbers, that is, it has good income, and knows how to correctly manage its expenses, the company has excess cash.

That is, the company makes a profit.

And why is this important?

Because if you plan to work in a company, it is important that you see its financial statements, to see if the company is profitable, and is a good place to work, or on the contrary it has financial problems, and unpaid bills.

.

You can see if a company has a good financial position or no,t by looking at its Financial Statements.

The legal part is also important, since there are some laws, regulations and taxes, which determine how much the company must pay in terms of taxes, which can reduce the profit margin of some companies.

FINANCIAL STATEMENTS FOR COMPANIES AND BUSINESSMEN

For entrepreneurs, it is very important to keep track of their financial statements, so they can know how their income is going, and their expenses, what they can improve to obtain better income, and what they can do to reduce their expenses without damaging the quality of the product. or service they provide.

The entrepreneur also needs to have solid financial statements, since they help them obtain financing from banks or other investors.

If you still do not have a company, and you have a business plan, the financial statements that you will project are important, you must also be very conservative to achieve your promises, to return the investment, to those who finance you and generate wealth for them.

FINANCIAL STATEMENTS FOR INVESTORS

The Financial Statements are also important for investors, since it is the way they evaluate businesses.

If the company is still in the project or business plan phase, the investor will see its projected financial statements, and its cash flow projected, which are possible income that this company will have in the future.

In some cases these projects are projected to return investment to investors in 2 to 5 years.

Sometimes in business plans, for example, your cash flow shows, for example, $ 20,000 of monthly income, and when the business is brought to life, this same company could have a real net income of $ 1,000. -1,000 $ which is a negative cash flow, that is, the company presents losses, which does not contrast with what was projected, causing investors to lose a lot of money, and be very careful when investing.

They'll be investing with trustworthy people, who know about the business, and who present realistic financial statements, projected from pessimistic, normal and optimistic scenarios.

If the company is incorporated and already has income, perhaps it needs a little more capital to grow and expand, in this case you have to evaluate if the company is capable of facing its debt, and you do this by looking at its surplus money, its sales, and the expected growth of the company.

FACTORS THAT CAN MAKE A SUCCESSFUL BUSINESS

After reviewing various bibliography, I can mention a few, that mention some factors that could make a business successful.

-Management - The management skills of business owners is essential to guide the company.

-Management skills of business owners - The greater your managerial skills, the more tools you will have to carry out your business (knowledge of marketing, laws, technology, personnel management, cash flow management, ability to obtain financing, etc.)

-Momentum - technological moment- For the case of innovative companies in the technology area, this is very important, and let me explain it to you in more detail.

For example, it is recorded in various ancient bibliography that the Vikings arrived in the American continent (in the northern part) long before Columbus, it is also possible that other cultures have reached the American continent.

However, when the Vikings arrived in America, they could not conquer it, because they encountered hostile inhabitants, whom they could not defeat, because the weapons of both groups were similar.

So they chose to leave that land.

Most likely, the Nordics have discovered North America due to its proximity to Iceland and Greenland, which they did conquer.

Hundreds of years later, Columbus would arrive in America, and would manage to conquer it due to his technological superiority in weapons.

The Spanish had the arquebus, iron armor, iron swords, while the locals had sticks or mallets or knives to defend themselves.

That is why the technological moment is important.

Another example of this is, for example, the video transmission that YouTube took advantage of.

Since ten years before, other companies tried to do the same, but because the transmission of megabytes offered by telecommunications companies at that time was very little, it did not allow the transmission of videos fluent, or made it look choppy.

Momentum is important, and you can take advantage of it.

An additional example is Microsoft, which created Mixer, long after Twitch and Facebook Gaming, as these 2 giants already had a good part of the market, Mixer could not attract this audience and perished, it could be said that he arrived very late to the party.

It would be easy to say that there is a recipe for making any business a success, and there is a 100% guarantee of success, but this is not the case in real life.

Even large companies fail when they try to enter new markets or create new products.

For example, this is the case of Amazon in China, it was not successful, and had to close its operations.

However, Amazon is still one of the largest and most important companies in the world.

An important factor that can reduce the risk of bankruptcy, and increase the risk of success, is the determination of the entrepreneur and his ability to take risks and overcome obstacles.

A LITTLE OF TAXES

Taxes are born due to the need to contribute to the collective good, the so-called rule of law.

We all contribute to have clean firefighters, social security and parks.

The (Peruvian) political constitution protects the right to property, but by paying taxes, we are giving a part of our wealth and property to the state, which violates our right to property and wealth.

That is why any tax created is regulated by law, that is the principle of legality.

Since the tax affects our property, it can only be created by law and this is called the principle of legality.

Laws in Peru are dictated by the congress, which is made up of congressmen, here is the importance of choosing good congressmen, since they are the ones who will issue laws on tax matters, and they represent us.

Therefore, if Congress increases taxes, or creates new taxes, it is because in theory it is what we all want, because they are the ones who represent us.

Ideal Capacity - Because congressmen are the ones who make laws, on important issues such as taxes, and many others, a congressman must have suitable capacity.

In other words, he must be at the height of his position, and he must have the ability and adequate education for such position.

As I write this, in my country Peru, there have been numerous scandals of our congressmen, among the following: gold laundering, money laundering, ties to drug trafficking, ties to human trafficking, ties to cable / internet theft, pimping, etc. .

Congress represents us all, and Congress is the one that can raise or lower the tax, or create a new tax.

As I write this, nationwide political scandals, corruption, illicit enrichment, etc. continue to occur.

Before which the following questions arise in Peru:

Should we keep paying taxes? Should we pay more taxes even after so many political scandals?

With my professor who is an expert in tax matters, we talked about the suitability requirements for politicians and congressmen in our country, we came to a conclusion, if the requirements to choose good candidates (suitable capacity) did not change, then we citizens should choose well.

For this reason a good education is vital, it is not convenient for corrupt politicians to have an educated people, because an educated people begins to ask questions, they begin to question whether the things that are done are the best that could be done.

They prefer no one to ask questions, and people usually don't ask when they don't understand something.

Only people who know the topic being discussed can ask questions, topics such as accounting, law and ethics are important.

That is why education in legal, accounting and ethical matters is vital, that people know these issues.

People who know this issue is people that is difficult to deceive.

How can you tell if a country's public treasury is bankrupt? How can you know if the promises of politicians are viable?

Looking at its laws and its Financial Statements, to see the complete picture you need both tax and accounting knowledge.

I debated with my professor, a great expert in taxation for more than 15 years, the following.

Are the taxes exaggerated, are taxes too much?
We will explain it by explaining the following principle:

PRINCIPLE OF NON-CONFISCATORY

The constitution (Peruvian) establishes that the right to

property must be respected, but when a tribute is created, part of your property passes to the state.

For this reason, taxes can only be created by mandate of law, and it must not exceed certain limits.

A tax is considered confiscatory when its amount is equivalent to a substantial part of the value of capital, income or utility, or when it violates property rights.

But the constitution does not establish what that limit is.

Currently in Peru companies pay 29.5% Income Tax (IR), for some entrepreneurs it seems high.

So, we come back to the question: Are taxes a very exaggerated payment?

My teacher explained the following to us:

"As long as the person pays the tax, there is no confiscation, because he is paying the tax, that is, he is voluntarily accepting that it is not confiscatory"

There are other countries that pay much more taxes, but my teacher remarked: "Yes, but they are other countries", taxes between 50-70% are normal in other countries, but they are other contexts, different from the reality of Peru.

So why pay 29.5%?

The point here is, how much is finally left to the taxpayer, since companies have to cover costs such as: labor costs, social costs, corruption (in some countries), justice, none of them are free.

In some constitutions it is established that it is confiscatory when it exceeds 33.33%, in my country it is not clearly established, from which amount it becomes confiscatory, **but as I mentioned as long as the taxpayer pays and does not claim it is not confiscatory.**

The funny thing is that, in my country, there were marches of all kinds, but I still haven't seen a single march against paying more taxes.

For this reason, I once again emphasize that financial education, and including education in the legal and accounting area, are vital for any person, city and country, who wants to be able to face their problems and challenges in the present and future.

WHAT TAXES REFLECT

Taxes are paid because they reflect economic capacity.

And there are 3 indicators of economic capacity:

-Rent

-Heritage/Patrimony

-Consumption

Based on these 3 indicators, taxes are created, and among them we have:

- property tax (heritage)

-capital gains tax (equity)

-income tax (income)

-Vehicle tax (equity)

-General sales tax (consumption)

-selective consumption tax (consumption), among others.

The constitution of Peru establishes that property must be protected, and each time a tax is created, it must be seen how it affects the citizen's assets, and if it is confiscatory or not.

I wanted to cover this topic in the book, because taxes are part of our life, in fact, all our lives we will be contributing with our taxes, so it is important to know why we pay taxes and not just pay them for the sake of it.

As an employer, worker, you will also pay or pay taxes, but you have to know why we pay taxes.

At the beginning, countries like the United States did not pay taxes and people traveled to this country to enrich themselves. Famous events such as Boston tea were promoted with the intention of not paying taxes.

 Taxes were created, to extract money from the rich, in the same Robin Hood style, but then they affected the middle class and the poor class, and they are currently the ones who pay the most taxes.

As an entrepreneur, many expenses can be deducted, before paying taxes in a legal way.

This is what makes the rich richer in the long run, since many entrepreneurs buy assets before paying taxes, that is, they spend before paying taxes, while the worker can only invest after paying taxes, and this does all the difference. (It is advisable to consult a tax advisor, to see what is legal, and what is illegal, in this book we fully recommend working legally).

Another additional detail, which is worth mentioning here, **is when I asked my law professor about property and the principle of non-confiscation.**

I asked him the following:

- I recently read that an Anglo-Saxon country (I don't remember the country very well but I remember I read it in a best-seller book**), that if you don't pay your property tax for several months, the state takes away your property.**

Is it the same with Peru?

-And he said NO, here you cannot pay your property tax (property tax), **but your house is your house, you can rest assured that they won't take it away from you.**(If you owe property taxes)

Of course, he wasn't recommending not to pay, and me either.

But I mention this, because it's important to know that every person has the right to property and wealth.

There is a powerful phrase I have it in my mind, and it is from Thomas Jefferson and is the following one:

"… the banks and corporations that will grow up around them will deprive the people of all property until their children wake up homeless on the continent their Fathers conquered…"

I will add to this, the congress and the politicians, can also make us homeless, by creating new laws, that violate our right to property and wealth.

If we don't say anything when a new law is given that could be confiscatory, then we are agreeing with them.

If we don't say anything as my law professor said, then is not confiscatory, because **as long as the taxpayer pays and does not claim it is not confiscatory.**

As I said, the constitution protects the right to property, and we also have the principle of non-confiscation, in which the right to property is protected.

In Peru there are many people who are not up to date in the payment of their property taxes, but in the event that the person wants to sell their property, they must be up to date on all payments.

Therefore, many times, when a property purchase / sale is made, the bill is signed first, in this procedure the buyer gives a part of the total to the seller, this so that he pays the property tax that he owes in some cases, plus others like additional paperwork.

Once these tax payments are regularized, the public deed is finally carried out for the buyer, the property is registered in his name, and the property is formally transferred to his name.

I touch on the subject of taxes, since around our life, we will always be paying taxes.

Taxes are an important part of society, but also every person must protect her wealth and assets if he can do so legally.

Since as I mentioned again, we all have the right to property, and wealth.

IT'S NOT ALL MONEY

IT'S NOT ALL MONEY
"The man with a new idea is crazy until he succeeds"
MARK TWAIN

What is needed is creativity, vision, and persistence to achieve your vision, your idea, your business.

Many people have great business ideas, ideas that could make millionaires, but never execute them, the world is full of many people with great ideas.

Most people have great ideas, and sometimes they need capital to realize those ideas, it can be $ 5,000, $ 10,000, , $ 20,000, $ 50,000 to realize their business idea.

For this reason, they usually say: "I don't have money", I need money to start this company and that is where their dream ends, their mind closes to the possibility of undertaking it, and there ends all.

But if you watch and study carefully the history of millionaires, none of them started with a lot of money, or I need money to make money,

If they didn't have money, they looked for investors, if they didn't have the product, they looked for someone who did, if they didn't know something, they looked for help.

We will explain below the history of great entrepreneurs, who, with great cunning, intelligence and negotiation skills, achieved great feats:

CHRISTOPHER COLUMBUS'S STORY

After the fall of Constantinople, Europe could no longer trade with the eastern countries.

Columbus's hypothesis based on alternative and erroneous calculations about the size of the earth (he assumed it was smaller than it really was), made him believe that it was possible to reach Asia, by other means.

Columbus sought patronage and offered it to King Juan II of Portugal, who when consulting him rejected Columbus's offer, which made Colon emigrate to the kingdom of Castile.

On emigrating to Castile, he made friends with Fray Antonio de Marchena and years later with Fray Juan Pérez, to whom he entrusted his plans.

The friars recommended him to Fray Hernando de Talavera, confessor of Queen Isabel I of Castile.

The sovereign was interested in the idea, but she wanted a council of learned men to give an opinion on the viability of the project, while she assigned Colon, poor in resources, a grant from the crown.

Columbus in turn proposed his project to the Duke of Medina Sidonia who rejected it, and later to Luis de Cerda, Duke of Medinaceli, who was interested and welcomed Columbus for 2 years. But said to delay the project until the conquest of Granada.

In December 1491, Columbus arrived in Granada, and the project was rejected again, the opposition was due to the excessive demands of Colon.

The coffers of the monarchs after the war of Granada, were not going through their best moments, that is why Luis de Santángel, ration clerk, offered to lend the money that corresponded to contribute to the crown.

As you can see, a truly capitalist spirit, both on the part of Christopher Columbus and on the part of his investors who did not have much money at the time.

As you can also see, Columbus did not let money limit him, and making use of his business skills, he was persistently selling his idea to conquer Asia.

Columbus did not let the lack of money limit him, a very common excuse of people is that they do not have money to invest, but in reality money is not needed to make money, we can also see that their investors the kings of Castile, despite who had limitations at the time, financed Colon.

In short, pure capitalism, at this time and moment in history.

Today nothing can be compared with the discovery of America.

Not even the conquest of Mars. Although the conquest of Mars would be a great advance in technological terms, it cannot be compared with the discovery of America in economic terms.

Because when the American continent was conquered, all the wealth of the American continent, was transferred to Europe, besides that the American continent was bigger than Europe , and it was rich in minerals and natural resources.

The American continent had inhabitants, great resources and a large territorial extension.

Mars has none of the 3. If we were to conquer Mars, we would send resources to Mars, instead of extracting resources from Mars.
Mars is smaller than Earth. As I write this, Mars is considered a lifeless planet.

The discovery of the American continent is one of the greatest discoveries in history. And as I explain in economic terms, not even the conquest of Mars could be compared with the discovery of America.

Today in the American continent, more than 1,000 million people live, more than the 700 million who live in Europe.

Europe has 10 million km2 in territorial extension, the American continent has 42 million km2 of territorial extension.

STEVE JOBS

Steve Jobs, when he went to a company that manufactures technological products, he managed to see that they had a very small 1 gigabyte memory, still no one had any idea what to do with that memory, but Steve Jobs turned on his focus.

All that memory can be used to store and listen to music! from an iPod !, the iPod at the time revolutionized the world of music and made millions could carry in their pocket, not just one but hundreds of songs.

Later when he saw a company that had Touch technology, he went and said wham! This could be used in cell phones, and so he created the first touchscreen smartphone, the IPHONE, and again rocked the phone and mobile industry.

The ability to put objects together, technology, to create wonderful products was a Steve Jobs quality.

As well as the quality of him to sell, negotiate, and inspire others.

When he spoke at his lectures about the new introduction of the Iphone, the ipod, the ipad, he literally inspired people, and they were eager to buy Apple products.

BILL GATES

Bill Gates, negotiated the Windows operating system, when he did not even own the operating system, he asked IBM for $ 50,000, and with that $ 50,000 he immediately went to his friend Tim Paterson, to offer them for the purchase of the MS-DOS operating system.

Again the story of the entrepreneur who unites products, people (investors, workers, etc.), and tools to create a company.

MY BUSINESSMAN FRIEND

I have a businessman friend, with whom I usually talk at lunches and meetings, he is a successful businessman, with several businesses in different fields, he started out as a guitar singer, with his guitar, he went from city to city playing music making a living.

He told me several of his anecdotes, and one of them has to do with the subject of this chapter.

My friend, he often interacts with lawyers, accountants, and businessmen.

One day one of his friends, owner of a 500m2 commercial space, asked him if he wanted to rent it, the price was $ 2,000, at that time he did not have much money, but he told him that he was going to rent it anyway.

Then he called another friend who had the money, to show him the opportunity, the friend was interested in the place, but he needed his wife to see the opportunity, to make the decision, when the wife saw the place, he also agreed.

So they took the premises for rent (he generated the contract, the friend paid for it and they divided this venture

50-50), later they sublet it to several tenants, finally they managed to sublet the premises at $ 3,000 among several tenants. This commercial premises is in a tourist area in the city of Cusco-Peru, for which they sublet small spaces to small merchants, so that they can sell their products and crafts to tourists.

They had $ 1,000 left, so the winnings were divided at $ 500 each.

If my friend had limited himself, and said that he had no money, he would have missed the opportunity. Later he was given the opportunity to buy the commercial premises for $ 50,000 at that time, today that property is worth at least 5 million dollars, since at least 20 years have passed since that event.

In a way, passing the barrier from "I have no money" to "I will find a way to make it possible" is the litmus test of the business man.

Those who pass this "I have no money" test are strong entrepreneurs, with a strong mentality, who know that if they want something, nothing and no one can limit them.

These entrepreneurs are like the puss in boots, they find something, and they put the pieces of the puzzle together, they have the business idea in mind, they find the investor who will finance them, they gather the people they need to get the business going, basically they do what! whatever it takes! to get your business up and running and be successful.

They have a powerful mindset, they know their thoughts and words and they respect them.

And besides, none of them, let money (or lack of time or whatever) be a limitation to achieve abundance in their life!

Well, so far we have treated the stories of many entrepreneurs.

Maybe you have a great idea, but you don't have the money to make it come true, but as you saw that is not a limitation, there is a solution, and the solution may be investors willing to invest in your idea.

As you saw Colon, he looked for investors, and the kings of Spain helped him.

My businessman friend, he sought help and got funding from a friend.

Today, any self-respecting entrepreneur who is serious about doing business and obtaining financing can do so with a solid business plan.

Remember that if the idea is good and the business is profitable, there will always be someone willing to invest in that business.

Also the entrepreneur, to reach other people, must be able to convince others that his idea is good, and this is done by knowing how to SELL and being an excellent communicator.

If Columbus had not been an excellent communicator and salesman, perhaps he would not have convinced the queen, the greats are entrepreneurs are great communicators.

Also, if he hadn't had vision, and persistence, we wouldn't know him nowadays.

SOME STORIES OF STRUGGLE AND SUCCESS

I am Peruvian, and I want to share with you, some stories of success of Peruvian entrepreneurs.

I worked as a credit advisor for small and medium-sized companies, my work basically consisted of going from market to market, from business to business, to offer loans to entrepreneurs so that they could grow, I offered credit for working capital, fixed assets and for consumption .

I realized something, that many undertook with little or no capital, I know, for example, a person who did not have a single cent, only had his National Identity Document (DNI), what he did was, leave his DNI, which in Peru, has a value of approximately $ 5, in a neighboring winery, and exchange it for products such as soft drinks, sweets, cookies valued at that price.

Then he went to the markets, the streets, businesses, offering the sweets, he came to sell everything, and then he recovered his capital, recovered his ID, and returned with an additional profit, today he is a great winemaker.

He started because he had no other option, he knew that by not having an education he would not have found a well-paid job, so his only option was to start.

I know the story of another businessman (that was counted to me when I was in microfinance training), who was an assistant in a restaurant, and had the function of peeling potatoes, until he was fired, several months later, with several bills to pay, and on the verge of despair, he was filled with pity and self-pity , and in her tears he said:

"It is that I did not have the opportunities, I could not study at the university, I cannot find a good job, it is difficult to survive with such a low income, and I ONLY SERVE TO PEEL POTATOES, he complained while crying.

But while he cried he thought and thought, after several hours of crying and self-pity, he stopped feeling sorry for himself and then he said ZAS!
I ONLY SERVE FOR PEELING POTATOES !!!!

The next day he started his potato peeling business.

He went from restaurant to restaurant offering the potato peeling service, they rejected him at the beginning, until he managed to convince a businessman to work with him, he convinced him by saying that he was going to reduce his personnel expenses, he said the following "I can peel the potatoes, so your staff can take care of other more important tasks such as serving customers among others so you will save, spend less on staff and your staff will be more productive. "

He managed to convince him.

Today he is a great businessman. With many clients to whom he outsources his potato peeling service.

I also remember a businessman who was selling chickens, how did he start?

He only needed a table, a wholesale supplier who gave him 5 chickens on credit, and a small space that some relatives gave him near a commercial market, with what he sold, he reinvested and reinvested in his business, and today he is a great businessman, with several business stalls selling chicken.

And so there are hundreds of stories of small and medium entrepreneurs, and some today are known, such as the king of potatoes, the king of onion, the king of cheese, since they sell tons and tons of these products.

That is the reality of Peru, many people do not have a university education, they know that without a university education they will only be able to find a job with the minimum salary, therefore, if they want a better life, they only have to undertake, to obtain a better future and a better life.

None of them started his business because they had money left over, on the contrary, they started because they lacked money, but they had a dream, to get their family forward, to be successful, to succeed.

In the world in general, there are 2 reasons to undertake:
- entrepreneurship by necessity
- entrepreneurship by opportunity

These entrepreneurs out of necessity, often without formal education, do not open their law office, or their accounting firm, many of them start selling on the streets, or in small stores, and start selling products such as potatoes, fruits, vegetables, plastics, selling food, businesses that do not require a profession, and they do it because they often have no other option if they aspire to have a higher income.

When I worked as a credit advisor, I was surprised by the entrepreneurial capacity of these people, some of them started with 50, 100 soles (1/3 of a dollar) of capital.

The point is this, being an entrepreneur is not easy, many choose this path because many times they have no other option, it is a hard path, where one's strength and determination are put to the test countless times, there is no safe harbor, there is no security of a steady income, not even of success.

The only thing they often have is a relentless will and desire to succeed in order to give a better life to their family.

As an answer to the question, I asked at the beginning, who are this 10% that owns 90%?

They are entrepreneurs, those who sell shares, who create assets called businesses, out of nothing, AND who use to acquire more and more assets, and who make the rich richer every time.

If you have reached this point, I wanted to thank you for your bravery, and courage, as well as for your willingness to succeed, that this book has been an investment to you, that the hours invested, help you to set the guidelines for a prosperous life, of abundance And success.

SUMMARY

This book talked about entrepreneurship, what characterizes successful entrepreneurs, and some success stories, we covered a part of taxes, mindset of an entrepreneur, and some statistics of business success and labor satisfaction.

Entrepreneurship is vital to capitalism, since it is entrepreneurship and companies that shape the capitalist countries in which we live.

Companies provide value and services to customers, and benefit all actors in society.

Entrepreneurship is vital for every country, that is why many countries promote it and offer important tools for entrepreneurs.

FINAL NOTES

If you arrived to this point, I want to thank you.

I hope this book was helpful to you, and give you some ideas to improve.

I would like you to give me a review, to see how I can improve and what you liked about the book.

THE BEST OF WISHES, AND MAY YOU HAVE SUCCESS!

ABOUT THE AUTHOR

Max Chahua is a Peruvian coach, and a CPA.
He has written books about languages, economics,
productivity, finance, Coaching and Accounting.
After working in the banking industry, and in the Real
Estate industry, and finally in the Accounting industry.
He began his consultant career, where he mentors
entrepreneurs in tax and fiscal matters.
He also loves technology, has taken courses and seminars
on digital marketing, has created applications available in
the play store, like "easy kana" to teach Hiragana and
Katakana Japanese, and "aprende quechua", to teach the
traditional peruvian language.
He offers courses where he teaches digital marketing,
passive digital income, and courses where he teaches how
to sell your products or services in automatic.

www.ingramcontent.com/pod-product-compliance
Lightning Source LLC
Chambersburg PA
CBHW070921220526
45467CB00004B/1497